BMW

MOTORCYCLES

US ISBN 1 84222 273 2
UK ISBN 1 84222 385 2

Executive Editor: Chris Hawkes
Art Director: Mark Lloyd
Picture Research: Sally Claxton
Production: Lisa French

Printed and bound in Italy

BMW

MOTORCYCLES

THE ULTIMATE RIDING MACHINES

KEVIN ASH

CARLTON BOOKS

C O N T E N T S

Introduction 6

Plates 001-128 22

Captions to plate section 150

INTRODUCTION

The first BMW motorcycle was the 1923 R32, whose boxer twin, shaft drive layout has been used ever since.

By the end of 2001 BMW will have produced around 1.5 million motorcycles since its first machine, the R32, was built in 1923. During this 78 years of near-continuous production, interrupted only by World War II, BMW's world motorcycle markets underwent a series of dramatic changes as economic and political circumstances affected what people wanted or could afford to buy, and at one stage even dictated what BMW itself was allowed to make.

Many, many more motorcycle companies failed than suceeded during this time, some through unhappy circumstance and others because they did not, or could not, adapt their designs and technology to suit the changing world around them. Yet BMW has survived, and quite amazingly considering how long it has been established, it even entered the new millennium as one of the fastest growing and most promising motorcycle companies in the world.

All the more ironic then that where the key to remaining in business appears to have been adaptability, the BMW name has been synonymous with one particular engine configuration throughout its existence–the horizontally opposed two cylinder, or as it's universally known, the boxer twin.

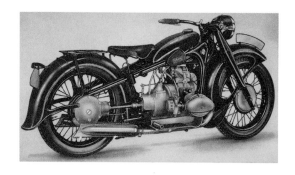

BMW has a long history of engineering innovation. In 1935, the R17 was the world's first production motorcycle with telescopic forks.

Of course there is more to BMW than simply an engine layout, just as there are more engine layouts to BMW. Hand in hand with that have been two other distinctive characteristics. The first is outstanding build quality, which if not always the actuality has certainly and importantly been perceived as a BMW trait. The second is innovation, mostly in the engineering but also on occasion in concepts themselves, although unfairly this hasn't always been the public perception of BMW, which to many motorcyclists is seen as one of the more conservative companies.

The quality aspects date back to BMW's roots, which originally lie in the aero industry.

After World War I, the Treaty of Versailles forbid BMW from building the aero engines for which it had been formed to design and manufacture (the BMW badge represents a spinning propeller), so the company cast around for something else to busy its engineering workers and equipment.

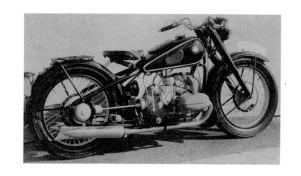

BMW's build and design were outstanding—the 1936 R5 is considered one of the finest bikes of the 1930s.

Consequently, by 1921, BMW was producing the M2B15 fore-and-aft boxer engine as a proprietary power unit used by many other manufacturers, but sales fell as customers began to produce their own motors, and the task fell to chief designer, Max Friz, to produce a complete BMW motorcycle.

Friz appreciated the virtues of the boxer twin, but turned it through 90 degrees to facilitate cylinder cooling and shaft final drive, and worked hard at overcoming the relentless reliability problems which had dogged so many contemporary machines. Inevitably perhaps, given Friz's aero design credentials and the company's aircraft

BMW's Georg Meier on his way to Senior TT victory at the Isle of Man, 1939, the first win by a foreign bike.

quality manufacturing equipment, the fruit of his work, the R32, immediately established a reputation for BMW for outstanding reliability with looks considered strikingly elegant. The company also positioned itself at the expensive end of the market, a region it has inhabited ever since.

By 1923, only the English company ABC had built a motorcycle with a boxer engine positioned with transverse cylinders, while the use of a shaft to drive the rear wheel had been attempted only by the Belgian company, FN. As with all the best ideas, though, it seems so obviously the right thing to do in retrospect.

In so many ways, then, the R32 encapsulated what BMW was to be all about from the outset. What surprises those whose experience of BMWs is only of more recent machines is the company's excursions into the field of competition and record breaking, something which began almost immediately with the R37, a racing derivative of the R32.

During the 1920s and 1930s the value of competition, and in particular record breaking, was enormous as a marketing tool for proving not just reliability but performance, which was a major issue in the years between the two wars. Winning foreign competitions against home-produced machines—always considered unbeatable by the partisan crowds—was a certain method of generating high-profile headlines and introducing a new name. After Rudolf Schleicher's gold medal win in the British International Six Days Trial in 1926, then one of the toughest international events, BMW became well-known in the UK. Two years later it was the Italians' turn to sit up and take notice when the German marque won the breathtakingly demanding Targa Florio. The victorious rider was one Ernst Henne, who went on to take a whole series of world land speed records during the 1930s, getting BMW's name onto the front pages of the mainstream national press in the process.

Racing certainly improved the breed as well as publicising it—in 1935 BMW introduced the R12, the first production motorcycle to be fitted with telescopic forks.

Come 1939 and BMW did the unthinkable by winning the Isle of Man Senior TT, the most prestigious international motorcycle race of them all and one which had never previously

been won by a foreign machine. Georg Meier was the rider who circulated the Island course

at a race average speed of 89.38mph, his pre-war, unfaired supercharged machine at times

exceeding 140mph.

After World War II, BMW stuttered back into motorcycle production, having

returned to its roots during the conflict to produce

aero engines and replenish its aircraft quality design

and build techniques in the process. The company

was flexible enough to understand the ubiquitous

post-war need for utility transport, but still a cheap

The 100mph R69 of 1955 was the first BMW to use Earles forks, and was noted for its sophistication.

BMW cost at least 50 per cent more than a cheap BSA.

In 1969, BMW released a new generation of boxer twin with a basic design which was to last into the 1990s.

While the rest of the world was busy adopting telescopic forks after the war, BMW was already moving on, fitting some, then all, of its bikes with the then superior Earles forks. It wasn't until 1969 that the Germans returned unreservedly to the by now far more sophisticated telescopic design they'd propagated.

This year represented something of a watershed in BMW's history, as the old range of boxer twins—the singles had already been phased out—was replaced in its entirety by the new /5 series. This upset the traditionalists, but set BMW up for an assault on the 1970s which was to prove so successful—it survived against the devastating Japanese onslaught which finished off so many other European manufacturers.

BMW stood aside from the horsepower and performance race to depend on the virtues of the boxer twin, at the same time as being fettered by its limitations. As the 1970s progressed, the attractions of four-cylinder engines—as so effectively campaigned by the Japanese—appeared to overwhelm BMW's faith in the boxer, and plans were formed to create a four of its own. The near-obsession with individuality, which probably more than any other single characteristic has been responsible for BMW's survival at the same time as boxing it in, ensured the German four would be like no other. Sure enough, come 1983 the new K-series machines arranged their engines in an unprecedented way. This compromised technical aspects of the motors, unquestionably, but still a BMW aficionado could choose a multi without following the crowd, and the popularity of the K-series—whose design modularity lent itself to the production of three-cylinder versions—set in motion a plan to phase out twin production altogether.

It seemed like a good idea at the time, but 1980 saw the beginning of an upheaval in western markets as the motorcycle-as-utility-vehicle gave way over the next decade to the motorcycle-as-leisure-pursuit. BMW almost casually invented a new class of motorcycle, the big capacity trail bike, with its R80G/S, a sort of two-wheeled Range Rover with at least as much influence as the iconic four-wheeler within its own sphere, but the direction motorcycling was heading was inevitable.

The 1990s motorcyclist was no longer the young, penurious refugee car driver, but an affluent broadsheet reader with time and money to spare. His requirements (and increasingly her requirements) had little to do with economy, more with hedonism, and as the performance of all motorcycles, Japanese and European, began to exceed the capabilities of the majority of riders, attributes such as style, individuality and character came to the fore.

Briefly (and we're talking months rather than years), BMW missed the direction the markets were heading and ceased production of its boxer twins altogether. The outcry brought it to its senses, though, and the old bikes were revamped while, concurrent with the K-series, a new generation of twins was planned in order to tap into the need for soul in a motorcycle which a two- or three-cylinder engine seemed able to deliver, where a four could only look on from the sidelines.

One of the great BMWs was the R90S of 1973 which matched fine handling and 120mph performance with genuine touring ability.

The boxer twin was reinvented in 1993 as the R1100RS, this time with fuel injection, the ABS brake system pioneered by BMW, yet another unique front suspension system—Telelever, with its wishbone and fork combination—to match the unique, single-sided, swingarm/shaft drive rear end, while the bike did without any main frame whatsoever.

Motorcycling's Range Rover, the 1980 R80G/S, created the big trail bike category and has set the standards ever since.

The arrival of David Robb as head of motorcycle design in 1993—by which time design had come to mean something linked to, but separate from, engineering—saw the technical innovation reinforced by styling and marketing originality. A simple question was asked—why did BMW only produce touring bikes? The answer was unconvincing, so

Robb tested the waters with dramatically different styling on the K1200RS which elicited a mostly favourable response, then entered an arena unthinkable for BMW: custom bikes.

Where almost every other manufacturer had found it necessary to produce its own safe but unimaginative take on the Harley-Davidson V-twin theme, BMW instead somehow contrived to produce an effective custom boxer twin with Telelever and Paralever suspension, the R1200C.

Come 2001 and BMW even showed that the ordinary, everyday, unfaired base model motorcycle—its new R1150R—could be stunningly attractive to look at as well as great fun to ride.

In 1983, BMW produced its first ever four-cylinder machine, the K100, with which it planned to supersede the boxer.

Intellectually, this unlikely broadening of BMW's range and uptake of new concepts, while retaining the company's core values, is enormously satisfying in itself, but the crucial bottom line, as the accountants see it, illustrates the stark commercial value: it works.

Sales of BMWs in the last decade have doubled, which is an undeniable vindication of the new-found boldness and a pointer to a future where BMW promises to continue mixing its policy of continuous development with genuine surprise. As former director of BMW's Motorcycle Division, Helmut Werner Bönsch said of Max Friz: "You will quickly find an astounding similarity with the

A decade after the K100 the all-new and highly innovative R1100RS was launched. The boxer twin was back!

development of organic life: in both cases we see a process of long-term evolution and then, all of a sudden, a rapid mutation, a quantum leap in development."

Quite what that next leap will be only BMW's engineers know, but as confirmed by the 2000 C1, the world's first two-wheeler with car-type, passive safety systems, the only thing you can expect is that it will be unexpected.

001

003

004

005

006

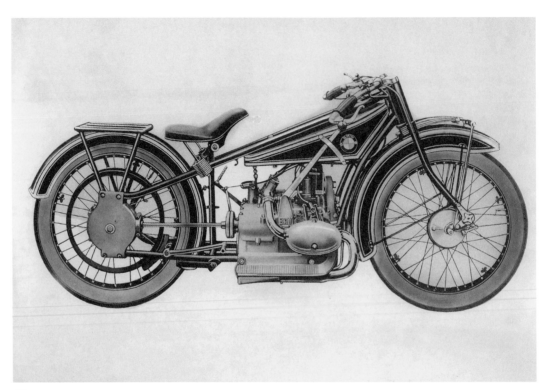

007

008

009

010

011

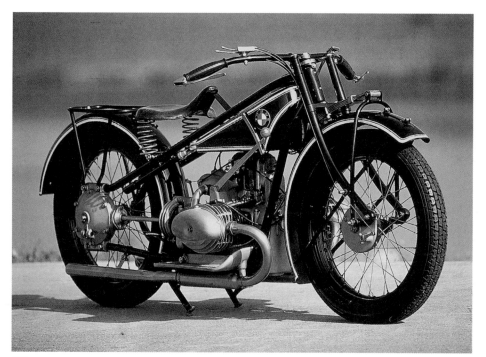

012

013

014

015

016

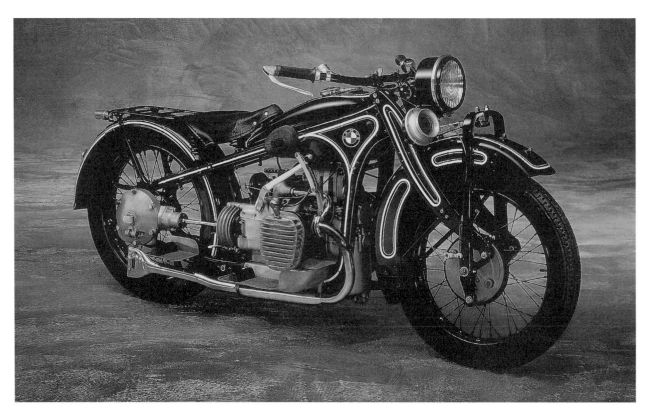

017

018

019

020

021

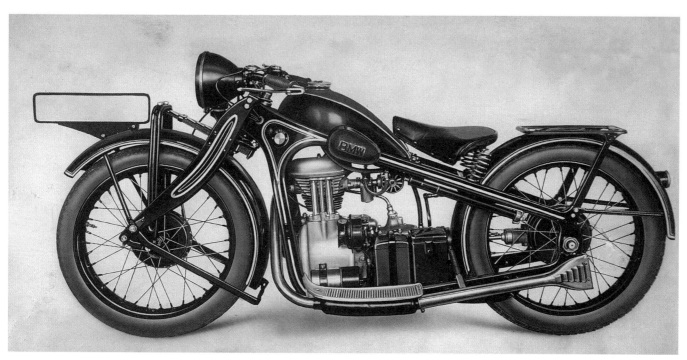

022

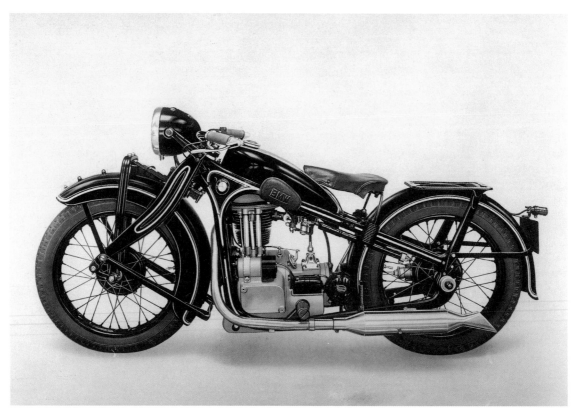

023

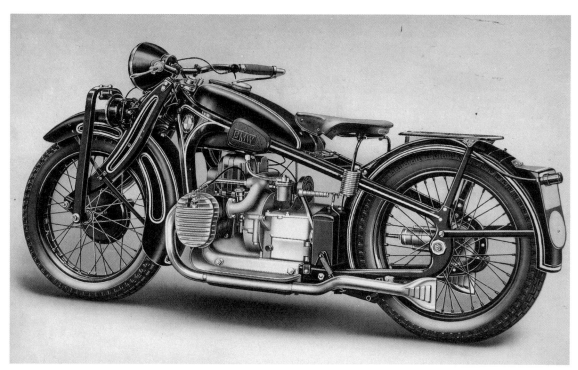

024

025

026

027

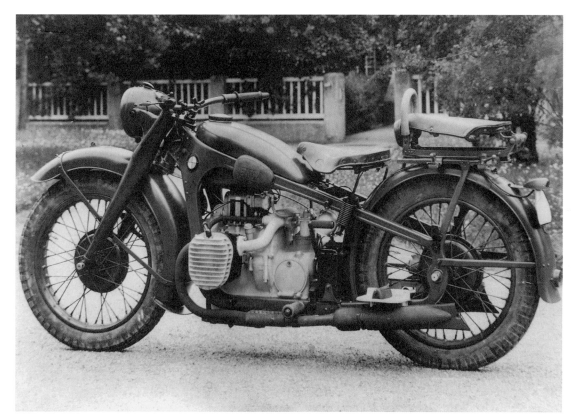

028

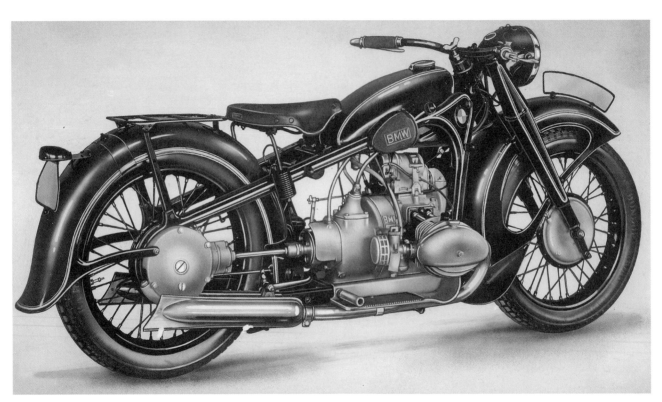

029

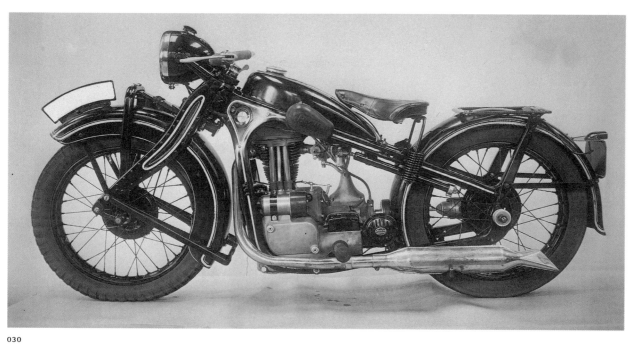

030

031

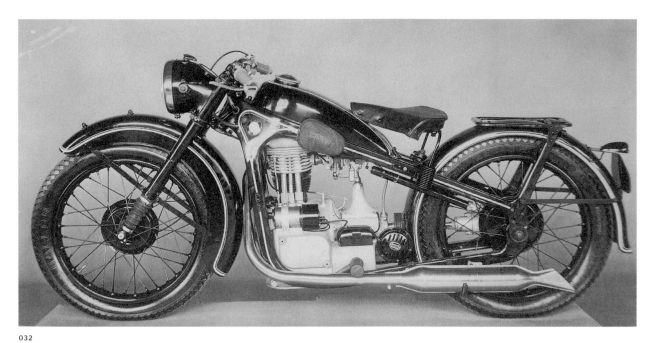

032

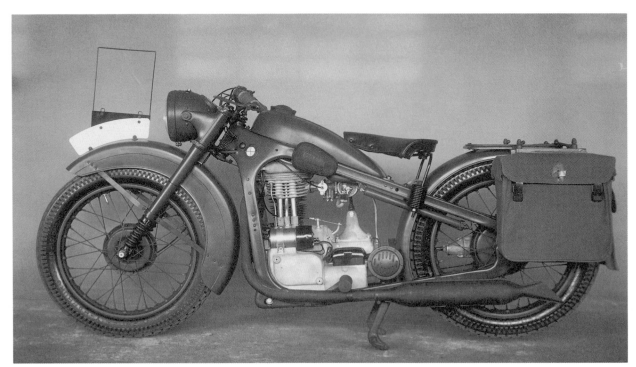

033

034

035

036

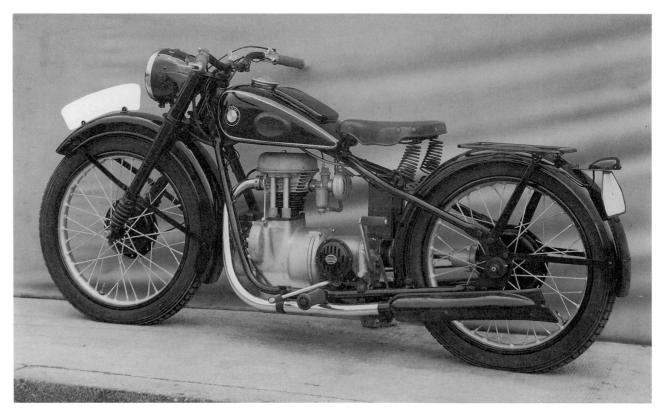

037

038

039

041

042

044

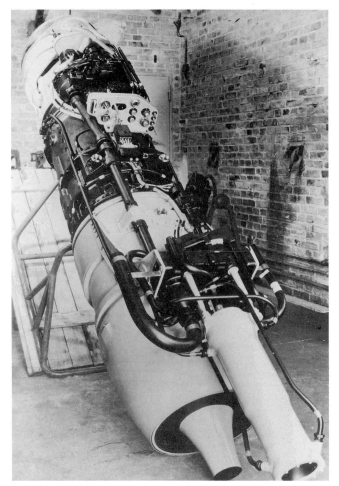

045

046

047

049

051

052

053

054

056

057

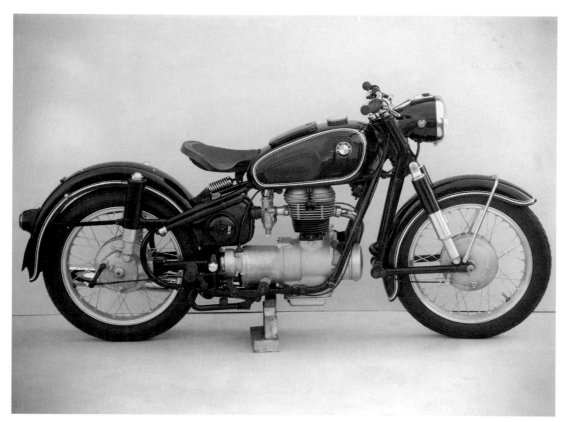

058

059

062

063

064

Dr. Quandt

070

072

074

081

082

083

084

085

089

093

099

103

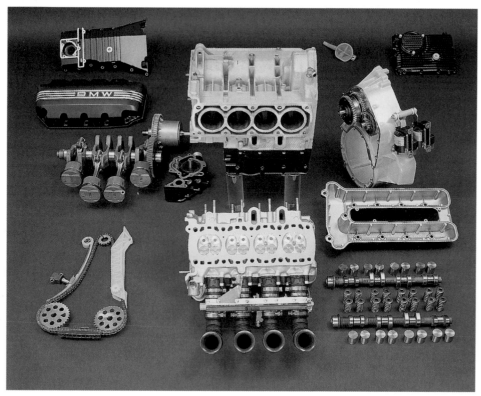

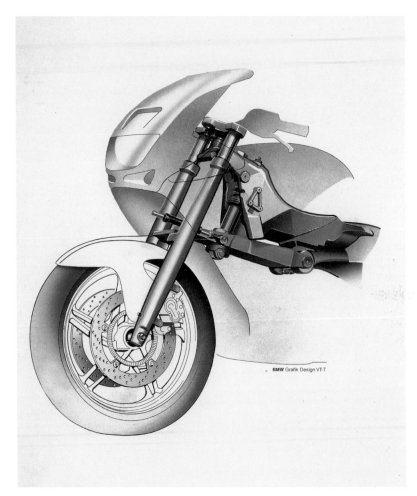

BMW Grafik Design VT-T

109

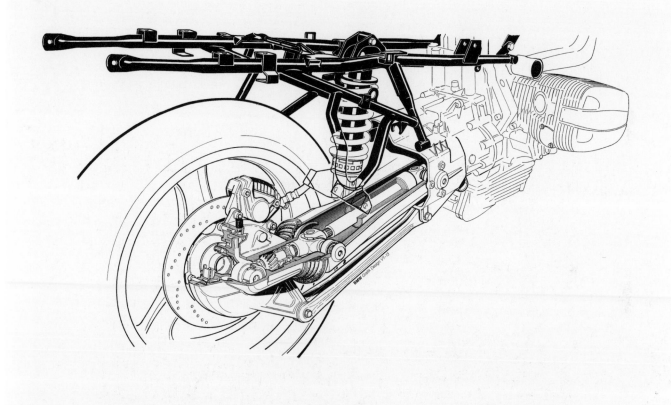

120

123

CAPTIONS FOR PLATES
001-128

001

Max Friz was originally an aircraft designer, working as chief design engineer in 1914 for Rapp Motorenwerke, which merged with Otto in 1916 to form BFW. This became Bayerisch Motoren Werke in 1917. German aircraft production was banned after WW1, so Friz reluctantly turned to motorcycles and designed the R32, the company's first bike. He retired in 1945.

002

Despite the Allied ban, Max Friz and BMW secretly produced this IV biplane which achieved the world altitude record of just over 32,000 feet in 1919. The Allies were furious and confiscated the plans, forcing BMW to look at other uses for its huge factory and engineering equipment.

003

Martin Stolle, center, worked with Max Friz on the first BMWs, helping develop the M2B15 494cc fore-and-aft boxer twin engine, originally a British Douglas design. This was a proprietary power unit used by many manufacturers, but it was the lessons learned with this which inspired Friz and Stolle to come up with the epochal transverse boxer twin used in the R32.

004

The R32 of 1923 was the first bike to wear the BMW badge, yet its basic configuration of shaft-driven transverse boxer twin has continued in almost uninterrupted production to this day. The first versions had only a wedge-block rear brake. The 486cc engine (increased to 494cc in 1925) produced 8.5bhp at 3,300rpm. Top speed was around 60mph.

005

From 1923 until production ceased in 1926, BMW built 3,100 R32s at its Munich factory. In these pre-production-line days each motorcycle was assembled from scratch to completion by the same small team, and it worked well as the R32 gained a reputation for exceptional reliability.

006

The 247cc R39 of 1925 was BMW's first single, effectively half a boxer twin with the cylinder moved upright. Bore and stroke dimensions of 68mm x 68mm plus many components were shared with the R32 and R37. Reliability was outstanding and performance very strong with a power of 6bhp at 4,000rpm and a 62mph top speed.

007

The R37 of 1925 was the racing derivative of the R32, although it was little more than a tuned R32 with the road equipment such as lights removed, although it featured overhead valves in place of the R32's side-valve design and aluminium cylinder heads. Only 175 were made in two years of production.

008

BMW's chief test engineer Rudolf Schleicher won BMW's first major trophy on this R37, taking a gold medal in the International Six Days Trial (ISDT) in Wales in 1926, then considered the toughest event in motorcycle sport. BMW factory entries also won silver and bronze medals. The bike produced 16bhp at 4000rpm, almost double the R32's power.

009

The R37 was enormously successful on the race tracks, winning around 100 events in Germany alone in 1925, including the 500cc class of the German Grand Prix, although this was not the blue riband event it is today. As well as the engine revisions, stopping was substantially helped by the addition of an expanding shoe front brake.

010

Josef Selzer, seen here on the R39 racer at the German Solitude circuit in 1926, won the German 250cc championship on the machine in 1925. In doing so he was instrumental not just in proving the R39's performance and reliability, but with his continued subsequent successes on bikes such as the R47 helped established BMW as a major manufacturer.

011

The R32 was eventually superseded in 1926 by the R42, a bike which represented an evolution rather than an outright replacement. This model development policy has been typical of BMW ever since. Power was increased to 12bhp at 3,400rpm and fuel consumption improved too. The rear block brake was replaced by a drive-shaft shoe brake. Lights were an optional extra!

012

The R47 of 1927 was the sporting option, superseding the R37. The leaf spring front suspension and overhead valves were retained, but power was increased by 2bhp to an impressive 18bhp at 4,000rpm. This was a full production model, with 1,720 machines sold in the two years it was built

013

The first production BMW 750 was the 745cc R62 of 1928, a touring bike rather than a sports machine with a side-valve engine producing 18bhp at 3,400rpm. The pistons were still being made from cast iron at this time, although the sporting R63 derivative of 1929 used aluminium ones. You still had to pay extra for lights.

014

The R52 of 1928 took over from the R42, effectively a smaller version of the R62 using the same 78mm stroke with a 63mm bore for unusually undersquare dimensions for BMW. The result was a 487cc capacity with a power output of 12bhp at 3,400rpm. Lower sidecar gearing was an option, which came with a stronger double-plate clutch.

015

The sporting R63 of 1928 was the first BMW to be tagged the "Golden Arrow" by the British press for its high performance, a name which carried over to the R16 which followed. It was more than just an R62 with overhead valves, as it had aluminium pistons and oversquare bore and stroke dimensions of 83mm x 63mm. Power was 24bhp at 4,000rpm.

016

In the 1920s and 1930s breaking world records was a highly effective way of generating mass publicity. BMW's most successful exponent in this field was undoubtedly Ernst Henne, who collected 76 records between 1929 and 1937. He's pictured here in 1929, gaining the mile record at 134.68mph on a supercharged 750 on the road between Munich and Ingolstadt.

017

The 745cc R11 went on sale in 1929, replacing the R62. The bike was distinguished by—and disliked for—its pressed steel frame, used for economic reasons. BMWs with these frames were known as "star framed" bikes, probably a corruption of the German "stark" meaning strong. Power was still 18bhp, but top speed only 62mph. Lights were standard, at last.

018

The star-framed R16 was the sporting stablemate of the R11, featuring a 736cc overhead valve, 83mm x 68mm engine. Power was 25bhp at 4000rpm, but weight was up 10kg (22lb) to 165kg (364lb) compared to the old R63. The bike became known as the Golden Arrow for its 75mph performance. Pictured is the final series 5 version, which now had twin carburettors.

019

The Targa Florio was a famously dangerous race in Sicily where BMW proved the value of supercharging its twins. BMW's first win here came in 1927 with Paul Köppen, followed by Ernst Henne in 1928. Köppen is pictured here in 1929 on his number 2 machine on the start line before making it a third win for BMW.

020

Ernst Henne's versatility appeared to know no bounds. As well as his multiple world records and various road race wins, he also competed in ice racing. Henne is shown here in 1930 on the supercharged 500cc twin modified with studded ice tyres. The supercharger (Kompressor in German) was made by Swiss company Zoller. Note Henne's insulated suit and warm overboots.

021

Ernst Henne in 1931 aboard a 750 Kompressor on the Munich–Ingolstadt road attempting to reclaim his world record from Joe Wright, who had topped the German's previous record of 137.58mph by covering a mile at 150.65mph on his Zenith-JAP in Ireland. Henne finally beat Wright in 1932 with a 151.77mph pass.

022

BMW produced its smallest motorcycle ever, the 198cc R2 introduced in 1931 (1932 model shown), to dip under a German 200cc tax limit. The world was in recession and even BMW had to look to the budget bike market, although the R2 was still expensive. The overhead valve, 6bhp engine was notable as the first BMW to feature a one-piece "tunnel" crankcase.

023

From 1932 to 1938 around 15,000 examples of the rugged 398cc single-cylinder R4 were made, many for the military which dictated the right-side kick start, unusual for BMW. The bike gained a four-speed gearbox in 1933 and power was increased by 2bhp to 14bhp for this 1935 series 4 model, although top speed was still a modest 65mph.

024

In total, BMW produced five versions of the R11 after 1929, a slow and steady development process which was to become typical of the company in between its short bursts of activity when whole new model ranges would appear. Pictured is the Series 4 model. As the R11 reached the end of its production, the single Gavernor carburettor was replaced with twin Amals, raising power 2bhp to 20bhp.

025

Ernst Henne and another world record attempt. Here he is at Gyon in Hungary in 1934 raising his own previous record of 151.77mph to 152.81mph on a 745cc Kompressor twin. Henne's attention to detail was meticulous—even his crash helmet and leathers were streamlined. Henne broke records until 1937 and was unbeaten until 1951.

026

Franz Josef Popp (pictured here in 1935) joined BMW in 1917 and soon became general manager thanks to his engineering background and management skills. His vision and leadership were the forces behind the creation of BMW's young and dynamic team of engineers, and it was his idea to apply aerospace standards to motorcycles. He retired in 1942.

027

BMW took its use of pressed steel in frames a dramatic step further with the 1935 R7, which had full monocoque bodywork supporting the steering head and rear axle. The bike was also notable as the first BMW to be fitted with telescopic front forks, but the machine was considered too radical and never went into production.

028

The R12 arrived in 1935 with essentially the same frame and 745cc side-valve engine as the R11 which it replaced. But it's a milestone in motorcycle history, as it's the first production bike to be fitted with telescopic front forks, for which BMW owned the design patent. Pictured here is the military version.

029

The sporting R17 introduced telescopic forks to the world alongside the R12 in 1935 (1937 model shown here). Other advanced features included interchangeable 19-inch wheels, a four-speed gearbox and twin Amal carburettors (made in Germany under licence). The overhead valve, 745cc, 33bhp engine spun to 5,000rpm and top speed was 87mph. The old R16's rigid, rear-end star frame was still used though.

030

The R3 of 1936 was closely based on the single-cylinder R4, its 305cc capacity achieved by reducing the bore to 68mm from the R4's 78mm. The stroke of 84mm was retained, as was the rolling chassis. Power and top speed were good at 11bhp and 62mph, but sales were poor and only 740 were made in the one year of production.

031

The innovative 1936 R5 was one of the great bikes of its decade. Features included telescopic forks, a steering damper and, making its BMW debut, positive stop foot gearchange. The twin cradle frame was tubular steel with exotic round and oval section combinations. The advanced all-new 494cc engine was now twin cam with a one-piece tunnel crankcase. Power was 24bhp at 5,800rpm.

032

In 1937 the R4 was replaced with the 342cc R35. Apart from its telescopic forks and fashionable 19-inch wheels, it wasn't greatly changed in order to appeal to the conservative military. Power was up slightly to 14bhp at 4,500rpm despite the 4mm reduction in bore to 72mm, while top speed was unchanged at 62mph.

033

The majority of the 15,000 R35s made during its three year production run from 1937 were military rather than civilian versions. It was to appeal to this traditionalist market that the bike retained the now old-fashioned, hand-change, four-speed gearbox with right-side kickstart and sprung saddle.

034

The 1937 R6 was the side valve version of the R5, aimed more at sidecar users, and it shared the R5's rolling chassis and much of the engine and transmission, although new bore and stroke dimensions of 69.8mm x 78mm meant capacity increased to 596.9cc. Power was a gentle 18bhp, but low rev torque was substantial.

035

Adjusting the rod-operated rear drum brake on the 192cc 1937 R20. Note the frame is now tubular steel but still there is no rear suspension. Even the telescopic front forks were crude, doing without hydraulic damping, while the foot-operated gearchange was not positive stop, meaning gears could be selected in any order.

036

One of BMW's most successful riders, Georg Meier, pictured at the 1938 TT, when the rising German star replaced Briton Jock West in the factory team. But this was not a great year for BMW at the TT: Karl Gall crashed out in practice while Meier's bike was left on the start line after a plug thread stripped.

037

In response to a new law allowing bikes under 250cc to be tax free, the 192cc R20 in 1938 was replaced by the R23, the only significant difference being an 8mm increase in bore size to 68mm to give 247cc. One other welcome change was the partial recession into the fuel tank of the toolbox, whose prominence on the R20 had caused some eye-watering injuries in sudden stops.

038

Georg Meier posing for photographers in 1938 on the non-supercharged 500cc race bike he used this year and in 1939. The bike is still fitted with a sprung saddle even though it also features plunger-type rear suspension, introduced on the race bikes a year earlier. Even with twin carburettors instead of a supercharger, top speed was around 120mph.

039

The sophistication of the R5 was further improved when in 1938 the plunger rear suspension previously developed on the race machines was added. The rear axle was mounted onto a telescopic shock absorber built onto the rear end of the frame, allowing about two inches of movement. The bike was renamed the R51, but was otherwise almost unchanged from the R5.

040

Like the R5, the R6 became the R61 with the addition of rear suspension. Similarly, the only other changes were necessary ones, such as the inclusion of a universal joint in the drive shaft and a new bevel drive housing and rear frame design. The prices of both bikes reflected their quality and sophistication, each costing up to double their British equivalents.

041

1938 was a busy year for BMW. Another new machine was the 597cc R66, which shared the R51's rolling chassis and transmission. The engine used a single camshaft and the side-valve twin's crankcases along with overhead valves and was the quickest production BMW to date. The 30bhp power output gave it a top speed of around 90mph.

042

The fifth bike to debut in 1938 was the R71, a bike designed to replace the R12. Peak output was just 22bhp at 4,600rpm, but the low power, high-torque engine was meant primarily for sidecar use. For the same reason, early versions were also fitted with a hand gearchange, although this was soon replaced with a positive stop foot change. This was BMW's last side-valve engine.

043

Georg Meier on his way to an historic Senior TT victory on the supercharged 500 BMW, which averaged 89.38mph throughout the race. This was the first foreign machine to ever win the Senior TT. The bike had a top speed thought to be around 140mph and produced close to 70bhp, a huge amount of power for the time.

044

The R75 of 1942 was produced solely for the military, and some 15,000 were made up to 1945. The bike had four forward gears plus a low ratio box, making eight in total, plus two reverse. The overhead valve, single cam 745cc engine made 26bhp and plenty of low rev torque. It was produced at BMW's Eisenach car factory.

045

Inevitably during WW2 BMW's resources and expertise were directed towards the war effort, and the company soon became an early pioneer in jet engine design and production. This prototype engine, called the 003, was running as early as 1942 and went into full production in 1943, although Allied bombing of the Munich factory caused serious disruption.

046

BMW returned to its roots as soon as the war started, by designing conventional aero engines. This is the 14-cylinder radial which powered the Focke-Wulf 190 fighter of 1942 which outperformed the British Spitfire with its 410mph top speed and 37,000 feet ceiling. By this stage of the war more than 35,000 people were working for BMW.

047

In practice the R75 was always fitted with a sidecar, whose wheel was also driven via a lockable differential. The 16-inch wheels were interchangeable and could take car tyres. Performance inevitably was sluggish as a fully equipped R75 outfit could weigh half a ton, but it was effective in mud and sand. The bulge on the tank is a large air filter fitted for desert use.

048

After the war, BMW was first banned from motorcycle manufacture then set a 60cc limit, before this was raised in 1948 to 250cc. The single-cylinder R24 was ready, an updated version of the R23 with particularly clean engine lines. As with all BMW singles until the F650, the crank was aligned along the bike with the dry, single plate clutch mounted on the back.

049

The R25, pictured in Pisa for a BMW publicity shot in 1950, was essentially an R24 fitted with plunger rear suspension, the first on a BMW single. The engine was the same overhead valve, 68mm x 68mm bore and stroke unit producing 12bhp at 5,600rpm, but performance was slightly down as the changes came with a 10kg weight penalty.

050

The R67 of 1951 was the first new twin produced after the war, along with the R51/3—it had taken longer to uprate the twins than the singles, and demand anyway had been for the cheapest utility transport. The 594cc engine used a gear-driven single camshaft and was generally modernized and tidied. The bike was designed mostly for sidecar use.

051

The engine R51/3 of 1951 received the same makeover as the R67 of that year, which also included an unprecedented 160 Watt dynamo (60 Watts was the norm) for vastly improved electrics including a stop light as standard. A lot of effort was put into keeping the electrics dry. Ignition now was by magneto. The 494cc twin produced 24bhp at 5,800rpm.

052

BMW advertised the R68 when it came out in 1952 as its first 100mph motorcycle, a performance achieved from a 590cc overhead valve engine producing 35bhp and revving to more than 7,000rpm. The bike was available either as a conventional road motorcycle or in "cross-country" guise, when it was fitted with a high level, two-into-one exhaust.

053

The R67/2 was a slightly upgraded version of the 1951 R67, and like the R68 was also available as a cross-country version, even when, as here, it was fitted with a sidecar. Although the bore and stroke were identical to the R68's 72mm x 73mm, a lower compression ratio with smaller Bing carburettors resulted in a more modest 26bhp at 5,500rpm.

054

While the R25/2 was only
slightly modified from the R25,
the R25/3 of 1953 was
substantially improved. Power
was up 1bhp to 13bhp, but with
a lot more mid-range torque,
which helped to endow it with
an impressive 74mph top speed
and improved suitability for
sidecar use, as seen here. The
forks now featured rebound as
well as compression damping.

055

Well-known, post-war BMW
racer, Walter Zeller, on his way
to victory at the German Grand
Prix at Solitude in 1953 on the
fuel injected Rennsport 500. But
by now the Gileras and Nortons
were proving superior. Even so,
BMW continued its innovative
approach to front suspension,
using a leading link design
which appeared on road bikes
within two years.

056

BMW excelled itself with the
1955 R69, a machine acclaimed
for its blend of performance and
sophistication. This was the first
road BMW to feature the new
Earles-type leading link forks
and revised diaphragm spring
clutch as well as various other
changes. The 594cc twin
produced 35bhp, as on the R68
enough for 100mph, but
handling and ride quality were
much improved.

057

Although BMW lost its Eisenach
car factory to East Germany after
the war, it began car production
in Munich, starting with a
modified version of the pre-war
luxury 501. But demand was for
small utility cars, which BMW
met with the three-wheeled Isetta
bubble car of 1954, an Italian Iso
design built under licence, famous
for its front-opening door and
feeble 250cc or 300cc power.

058

The R26 of 1955 was the first
BMW single to be fitted with
Earles forks (designed by
Englishman Ernie Earles), with
the odd trait of rising under
braking rather than dipping but
it much improved ride quality.
Swingarm rear suspension was
now fitted at the back with
more generous travel than the
old plunger type, and overall
comfort was transformed.

059

The BMW tradition of being popular with police forces was already established by 1955. These R69s were fitted with the large "dustbin" fairings seen briefly in racing before being banned, and drag as well as rider protection was greatly improved. But stability in crosswinds was poor so they weren't always popular.

060

The 1955 R50 replaced the R51/3 and received the same engine and chassis improvements—notably the Earles forks—as the contemporary R69. Power of the 494cc twin was up 2bhp to 24bhp giving a top speed of 88mph. The manual ignition advance on the right handlebar was popular with sidecar riders, as was the central friction steering damper.

061

For those riders after a softer option than the sporting R69, the 1956 R60 was introduced. This shared the 594cc capacity but produced just 28bhp at 5,600rpm, meaning that it struggled to reach 90mph. The R60 replaced the R67, the last of the old-type twins, and shared the R50/R69 chassis with Earles forks and swingarm rear suspension.

062

BMW did its best to encourage sales with special US versions of its machines such as this R69, with screen, panniers and extra spotlights. But sales of all the new, expensive big twins were low—less than 5,000 of the 600s were sold by the end of the 1950s as people turned to the new generation of cheap, small cars. Financial trouble loomed.

063

The production lines at Spandau, Berlin, slowed towards the end of the 1950s as sales dwindled and worldwide motorcycle markets shrank. But the downturn was remarkably fast—here, in 1956, the prospects still looked good, although sales were already falling, as some of the world's best motorcycles were produced as well as fine sports cars, the Isetta was selling well and BMW still possessed a strong aero engine division.

064

Walter Zeller in 1956 now faced MV Agusta as well as Norton, Gilera and others in the 500 Grand Prix class, but he gave way only to MV-mounted John Surtees to come second in that year's championship. The bike was notoriously difficult to master, with quirky handling due to the Earles forks which worked well on road bikes but less so on the racers.

065

In 1959 BMW's financial situation was so bad a takeover looked inevitable—a takeover by Mercedes was a likely prospect, which could have meant the eventual end of the BMW name. But the sale fell through after banker Dr Herbert Quandt provided substantial backing, sold the aero engine division and restored business confidence generally. The Quandt family still controls BMW today.

066

After Earles forks appeared on the R69, the company continued using them until the end of the 1960s. The horizontal tubes pivoted on the steered downtubes with their movement being controlled by a pair of shock absorbers. The principle is identical to twin shock and swingarm rear suspension. The penalty was high steered and unsprung mass compared with telescopic forks, but rigidity was better.

067

BMW's revival after the traumas of 1959 was helped by large police orders during the 1960s—here the Munich police are using modified 1960 R50s, painted white and fitted with the usual police accoutrements. The bikes were used for a range of duties, and ironically proved most versatile in cities increasingly clogged up by the very cars which so damaged BMW's sales.

068

The extended rear loop frame design was retained on BMW's new swingarm, so the twin shock absorbers were each mounted on the back of the loop half way up their bodies, as on this 1960 R27 single. A proper universal joint had by now replaced the flexible rubber connection used on the earlier plunger suspension machines, which would not have coped with the additional wheel travel.

069

The shaft final drive and suspension layout of the 1960 R50/2 and all the twins of the time was the same in principle as on the singles, with the shock absorbers being mounted onto the rear frame loop. An additional mounting to the mudguard at the top added strength and rigidity. The final drive bevel housing also incorporated the expanding shoe drum brake.

070

In 1964, the most successful of all BMW sidecar racers, Max Deubel with passenger Emil Hörner, won their fourth successive world championship. The pair, pictured here on their way to victory at Signpost Corner at the Isle of Man TT, also won at Spa, Belgium, this year and finished second in Germany and France.

071

A grid full of BMW outfits at the opening 1965 Grand Prix round at the Nürburgring. The marque's domination that year was total, with all of the top-ten places going to BMWs, a trend which continued right up to 1974 when the two-stroke König engines took over. Eventual champions were the Anglo-Swiss team of Fritz Scheidegger and passenger John Robinson, six points clear of Deubel-Hörner.

072

The 1960s ended dramatically with three new models for 1969 including the 498cc R50/5 (here with high-rise US handlebars). The engines were entirely new, with camshafts beneath the cranks instead of above while plain bearings and a high pressure oil system were debuted. Electrics were modern 12V, an electric start was an option. The frame was a Norton Featherbed-style twin cradle with conventional telescopic forks.

073

The biggest new 1969 machine was the 746cc R75/5, sharing the 70.6mm stroke of the R50/5 and R60/5, but with an 82mm bore. Power was 50bhp at 6,500rpm. Rear shocks were now mounted top and bottom. Some traditionalists mourned the passing of the old generation of bikes, others baulked at the big price increases, but the changes were undoubtedly needed.

074

Klaus Enders took the world sidecar championship an astounding six times between 1967 and 1974, partnered by Ralf Engelhardt every year but one. Here in the 1973 season their domination was absolute, as they won seven of eight championship rounds, finishing with a 27-point lead. Six of the top-ten machines were BMW-powered.

075

In 1973 BMW's sales were reasonably strong at around 25,000 annually, and the momentum was maintained with the /6 models replacing the /5 machines, although the slow-selling R50/5 was dropped from the range. The R60/6 featured five gears instead of four and the longer wheelbase of the last /5 models, as well as a smaller fuel tank and detail changes.

076

All attention in 1973 was focused on the R90S, another classic BMW. Engine capacity increased to 898cc thanks to 90mm pistons and the same 70.6mm stroke, with power up to 67bhp at 7,000rpm, good enough for a top speed of more than 120mph. The glamour was enhanced by the twin front brake discs, bar-mounted nose fairing and smoked edge paint finish.

077

Almost unnoticed at first alongside its headline-grabbing stablemate was the softer R90/6, although it proved just as popular as around 25,000 examples of each were sold in the next three years. Power was 60bhp at 6,500rpm, and a single front disc was fitted. Engine bottom end and most chassis components were common to the entire /6 range and the 90S.

078

The R75/6 arrived with the R60/6 but featured a larger fuel tank (although the optional smaller one is shown here) and for the first time on a production BMW, a front disc brake. Like the R60/6 the instruments were modernized, the sidepanels altered and other details changed which caused the weight to increase 10kg (22lb) to 200kg (441lb).

079

In 1976, BMW increased the bore size yet again, this time to 94mm for a capacity of 980cc in its new R100 engine which it fitted to its first fully faired machine, the outstanding R100RS. As well as looking good, the fairing provided exceptional weather protection and high speed stability. After a short period the bike also became the first BMW to have cast aluminium wheels.

080

The R100S of 1976 replaced the R90S, although at first it used a 65bhp version of the new 980cc engine, where the R100RS produced 70bhp. But from 1977 the R100S used the RS motor. The R100 series engine was distinguished externally by new rocker covers with four instead of two horizontal fins and on some models a black finish.

081

There was a softer option to the sporting S and RS models in the R100/7, which used a 60bhp version of the 980cc engine but which had a broader spread of torque better suited to touring. A single front disc was fitted. In a highly unusual move, purpose-made touring accessories such as Krauser-designed panniers and a screen were available directly from BMW.

082

At the other end of the new 1976 range from the R100RS was the R60/7, the 599cc version of the twin which replaced the R60/6, although the changes were relatively few. A separate tachometer was fitted—easier to read than the previous one incorporated in the speedometer—the switchgear was revised and the seat improved.

083

The traditional 750cc capacity was addressed in 1976 by the R75/7, which matched the ubiquitous 70.6mm stroke with an 82mm bore for a true 746cc. Power output was modest for the bike's 195kg (430lb) weight at 50bhp, produced at 6,200rpm. Like all /6 and /7 Series machines, the R75/7 used BMW's five-speed gearbox introduced in 1973.

084

The R75/7 lasted only one year and was replaced in 1977 by the R80/7, its capacity increased to 797cc after a bore increase to 84.8mm. Many BMW fans considered this the best expression of the contemporary boxer twins for its combination of torque and smoothness. Power was 55bhp at 7,000rpm, although some versions produced 50bbhp to meet German tax laws.

085

The Berlin factory had re-established itself by the late 1970s as a financially sound manufacturer forging its own path.

086

Two years after its biggest boxer, in 1978 BMW built its smallest, the 473cc R45, a machine aimed at a legally defined German horsepower category. But its 27bhp was too feeble for its weight—even the 35bhp foreign market version was considered very slow. The near-identical 649.6cc R65 launched alongside it was much more successful.

087

BMW wanted to cater for every type of touring rider and complemented the fully faired and well-equipped R100RT in 1978 with the far more basic R100T. This shared the same 980cc engine producing 70bhp at 7,250rpm, but at 198kg (437lb) it weighed a full 36kg (79lb) less and so performed considerably better. Owners would generally fit their own touring equipment.

088

BMW's plans for a four were well known in 1980, so the arrival of the innovative R80G/S (Gelände/Strasse, or off-road/street) was a surprise. The bike single-handedly invented the big capacity trail bike category and featured technical innovations such as all-aluminium, ceramic-plated cylinders and a single-sided swingarm with monoshock. The bike worked remarkably well both on- and off-road.

089

Alongside the imaginative R80G/S the effort to spruce up the R65 in 1981 looked uninspired, the R65LS falling somewhere between style and tradition while satisfying neither camp. The 650 twin featured an angular nose fairing with sporty low handlebars and a matt black finish on the exhaust system. Power was still 50 bhp at 7,250rpm.

090

The R100CS appeared in 1982 as a replacement for the R100S. The 70bhp engine was unchanged apart from using the more durable and lighter all-aluminium cylinders and the lightweight clutch which both debuted on the R80G/S. The CS stood for Classic Sport, a tacit recognition that the twins were now well off the pace of Japanese sports bikes.

091

The 1984 R80RT was subjected to the same improvements as the R80, and had become the flagship twin-cylinder tourer as the R100s had been deleted with the introduction of the K100. Despite, or possibly with some irony because of, the stifling effects of emissions laws, this particular incarnation of the boxer twin was considered by many to be the best ever for its balance of smoothness and power.

092

After the outstanding success of the R80G/S, BMW attempted to cash in with a more road-oriented version, the R80ST in 1982. The G/S's monoshock, single-sided swingarm and high-rise exhaust were re-used, but the suspension and wheels were purely road items. The result was a worthy but unexceptional machine.

093

The liquid-cooled, fuel-injected double overhead cam, four-cylinder K100 engine of 1983 was BMW's response to the Japanese, but to be different, the cylinders were horizontal and the crank was aligned along the bike, which facilitated shaft drive. Technically advanced in many ways the design was also compromised, using old-fashioned 67mm x 70mm long stroke dimensions and overly short conrods for compactness.

094

As much for the respect engendered by the badge as its performance, the 1983 K100 was a success, suggesting BMW's plan to phase out the twins was on course. Early examples suffered reliability problems, but these were corrected, while the high levels of vibration were mostly overshadowed by excitement at the boldness of the design. The chassis was all-new and incorporated the engine as a stressed frame component.

095

The model structure for the K-series followed the same pattern as for the twins. The K100RT of 1984, for example, was the fully faired touring version in the same mould as the R100RT, and as with the twins, so the K models proved popular with many police forces. They were particularly attracted by the substantial power advantage over the twins, the motor producing 90bhp at 8,000rpm.

096

With the K-series engine aligned along the bike, a big effort had to be made to keep the whole package short enough to fit within a reasonable wheelbase. BMW dubbed its engine and transmission design the Compact Drive System, the five-speed gearbox, clutch and shaft drive all being as short as physically possible. The single-sided swingarm with enclosed drive shaft was now the norm for BMWs.

097

In 1984, the stock K100 was joined by the sportier K100RS, distinguished by its slim fairing which reached down to the top of the engine. Power of the engine was unchanged at 90bhp, although the suspension was made firmer to carry the extra weight of the fairing and for sharper handling. More than half of BMW's production by now was of the K-series machines.

098

The civilian version of the K100RT further expanded the 1984 range and underlined the company's reputation for fine touring machines. The fairing, in particular, offered exceptional weather protection and the panniers now came as standard fitment. The engine's low rev torque particularly suited this role, although high rev vibration was well above average and gearchanging characteristically was clunky and slow.

099

Although BMW was gradually winding down twin production, new bikes in 1984 still showed several improvements. The base R80 featured the swingarm and clutch from the R80G/S with detailed internal changes which made it much smoother. Power was down 2bhp to 48bhp as emissions regulations tightened, but the bike felt more responsive than before.

100

The modularity of the K-series engine allowed BMW to introduce a 750cc three-cylinder version, which it did in 1985. The base K75C was the debut model and shared more than half its components with the K100, substantially reducing production costs. Revised cylinder heads meant more power per litre than the fours–75bhp at 8,500rpm–although cam timing and valve sizes were unchanged.

101

A year after the K75C came the K75S with a small, frame-mounted fairing, firmer suspension and a disc instead of drum rear brake. Although the engine was identical, top speed was up 6mph to 130mph due to the improved aerodynamics. The three-cylinder bikes were preferred by may riders for their sharper handling due to the reduced weight, and the less busy feel of the engines.

102

Following the pattern for increased luxury on touring bikes, BMW introduced the K100LT in 1987. The bike featured a large and very protective fairing as well as panniers, top box and even wiring for the fitment of a radio. The rear suspension was self-levelling to compensate for the expected heavy loads.

103

In the autumn of 1987, the R80GS (changed from G/S) gained Paralever suspension and a 980cc R100GS was added as BMW began the process of phasing the boxer engine back in. Production had halted briefly in 1986 as the company switched entirely to the K-series, but the outcry from enthusiasts made them change their mind. Meanwhile work began on an all-new twin.

104

Another first for BMW was the introduction of its electronic ABS anti-lock brake system on the K-series bikes in 1988. Via sensors on each wheel, a central computer could detect if a wheel's rate of deceleration exceeded predetermined figures. If so, the brake pressure would be released briefly then reapplied to prevent lock-up, and the process was repeated at around seven times per second.

105

The R80RT was another reintroduced old-type boxer, still selling alongside the K-series machines and in particular proving popular with police forces, the military and other large organizations for its ease of maintenance and reliability. Changes to the police bikes were relatively few, and included a more powerful alternator as well as a single seat unit and additional wiring for lights and radio equipment.

106

In 1989, BMW introduced a 16-valve version of the K100 engine in the controversially styled K1. The change to two inlet and two exhaust valves per cylinder, and an increase in compression ratio, boosted power to 99bhp, a ceiling voluntarily adhered to in the German market in the face of concerns about the growing outputs of motorcycles.

107

The K1's aerodynamic but bulbous styling caused a stir in 1989, especially as some garish colour schemes were used. The bike was billed by BMW as a supersports machine, although compared with the yardstick Yamaha FZR1000 EXUP it was both heavy and underpowered. As a GT touring bike it worked much better and did well in many countries. The 100,000th K-series was a K1.

108

The K1's 16-valve engine migrated into the K100RS in 1990, boosting power by a now much-needed 10bhp to 99bhp at 8,000rpm with torque rising too. The bike also benefited from the K1's Paralever rear suspension and importantly, its four-piston Brembo front brakes. The majority of K-series bikes were now fitted with ABS.

109

In 1990, BMW began work on the prototypes for a radical new front suspension system called Telelever, even though the telescopic forks pioneered on the 1935 R12 were now universal. The system comprised telescopic legs clamped in a single, pivoting upper yoke located just above the mudguard by a wishbone. Dive under braking was reduced by 90 per cent, but unsprung weight increased.

110

The first capacity increase for the K-series came in 1992 with the touring K1100LT, the 1,092cc capacity achieved by a bore increase to 70.5mm. Power remained at 99bhp, albeit at a slightly low 7,500rpm, but torque increased to 79lb.ft (107Nm) at 5,500rpm, against the K100RS's 74lb.ft (100Nm) at 6,750rpm. The rear shock absorber was sourced from Japanese company, Showa.

111

The F650 of 1993 was a sign of some radical changes in thinking at BMW. The liquid-cooled, 652cc, single-cylinder trail bike was the first BMW to feature chain final drive. It was designed in conjunction with the Austrian Rotax engine specialist and rising Italian company Aprilia, and meant BMW now boasted one, two, three and four-cylinder engines in its range.

112

Another first for the F650: no previous BMW had been produced outside Germany, but production was contracted out to Aprilia which ran a line dedicated to the F650 at its Noale factory. Although the bike was closely related to Aprilia's Pegaso the two bikes shared surprisingly few components. Despite the fears of BMW purists, the bike was outstandingly successful.

113

The all-new R1100RS of 1993 had many innovative features. The eight-valve, air-cooled, fuel-injected 1,085cc boxer designated the R259 engine had twin "high" cams sited alongside the valves, driven by chain from an auxiliary shaft below the crank, to minimise engine width. The radical Telelever front suspension and rear Paralever both attached directly to the engine. There was no main frame.

114

BMW's Paralever system was introduced in 1987 on the new R80GS, then modified as here for the new R1100RS boxer in 1993. The trapezoid geometry of the shaft housing and the torque arm beneath it altered the response of the rear suspension to changing power loads, reducing the negative effects on the handling. Two universal joints were incorporated in the drive shaft.

115

Demand for the older bikes continued into the 1990s. It was satisfied in 1994 by the R100R Mystik, a special version of the 1992 R100R, BMW's best-selling model that year. The 60bhp, 980cc engine had distinctive rounded valve covers and various cosmetic adornments, and became the last model to be made with the old engine, as production ceased at the end of 1995.

116

Alongside the 1994 Mystik BMW offered the R100RT, which was gently enhanced in 1995 and called the Classic (shown here) in deference to this being the final year of the old engine. It was available into 1996 as stocks ran out. The bike included heated handlebar grips, two-tone metallic paint and an "R100RT Classic" tank logo.

117

As the range with the old engines was phased out, so new eight-valve versions were introduced. In 1996, the R1100RT arrived as the flagship touring twin. The engine and transmission were identical to those of the R1100RS apart from an altered final drive ratio, and Telelever and Paralever suspension were used. The upper fairing was revised for sleeker looks in 2001.

118

The legacy of the 1980 R80G/S continued when in 1994 BMW introduced the chunky yet appealing R1100GS (1998 model is shown here). In many continental countries big trail bikes had been proving very popular as touring bikes and the bike soon became a top seller. But it was unusual in having a genuine off-road ability, despite its size and weight.

119

In 1997, the K1200RS grew to 1,171cc and output leaped to 128bhp. The significance of the bike went beyond this: the dramatic styling came from changes in attitude precipitated by design chief David Robb—if it had failed, the raft of subsequent bold new models pivotal to BMW's future direction would not have happened. Some markets, notably the UK, disliked the bike, but overall it did well.

120

David Robb had posed a fundamental question: why did BMW only produce touring bikes in the modern increasingly diverse market? The R1200C of 1997 and its 850cc sibling the R850C of 1999 underlined his doubts—BMW could produce a custom bike and tap into a lucrative sector new to it, yet still remain original and true to its principles. The biggest, wildest boxer was a great success.

121

The S suffix made a comeback on the R1100S at the end of 1998, after some 140,000 new generation boxers had been built in Berlin. The R1100S version was the most powerful boxer yet, producing 98bhp at 7,500rpm, and featured BMW's first six-speed gearbox plus improved Telelever. Top speed was 142mph, no match for the Japanese, but enough for many riders, and handling was exceptionally stable.

122

The 1171cc K-series engine was used in 1999 to power the luxury tourer K1200LT, aimed at Honda GoldWing buyers, but sleek and modern instead of the Japanese bike's 1960s style. Features included a reverse gear, integrated sound system, electrically adjustable screen and even optional heated seats. The bike handled surprisingly well for its size and comfort was outstanding.

123

In 2000, production of the F650 was brought back to the Spandau, Berlin factory from Aprilia, once the expansion programme was completed. The range of new models was proving more popular than even the most optimistic forecasts might have predicted, and production that year exceeded 70,000 units in a fast upward trend which was continuing strongly.

124

The company's innovation continued in 2000 with the C1, BMW's first scooter, first two-stroke and at 124cc its smallest engine. The roof was an integral part of the C1's passive safety system, which offered as much rider protection in some crashes as a small car. The C1 was aimed at car drivers after the congestion-beating ability of two wheels, but nervous of the increased risk.

125

In 2001, BMW introduced the R1150R to replace the R1100R, and showed that even a conventional, unfaired BMW boxer could be a stunningly attractive machine. It used the 85bhp engine from the R1150GS of 1999, notable for its wide spread of torque, and like all BMW new models since 1997, was fitted with a catalytic converter as standard.

126

By 2001, the dramatic boldness of design instigated by design chief David Robb in the early 1990s was paying great dividends in record sales figures. BMW was finally shaking off its staid, touring image and was replacing it with the near-heretic thought that its bikes could be sexy. In 1994, when this concept bike was shown, no-one thought it a vague possibility. In the new millennium, who knows?

127

In 1999, the GS series was uprated yet again when the R1150GS took over from the R1100GS. The 1,130cc engine had a bore and stroke of 101mm x 73mm, making it the biggest capacity trail bike ever produced by any manufacturer. But its popularity grew with it, and it was one of BMW's best-selling models, appealng mostly to touring riders despite the off-road style.

128

BMW's innovative approach continued in 2001 with the debut of its Integrated ABS system, which cleverly combined anti-lock brakes with servo-assistance for the first time on a production motorcycle. Each brake lever operates both front and rear brakes together, the rider's effort being enhanced by an ingenious adaptation of the ABS hydraulic pressure pump. The system even adapts to varying loads and road conditions.

PICTURE ACKNOWLEDGMENTS

The publishers would like to thank the following sources for their kind permission to reproduce the pictures in this book:

All photos: BMW Group, Mobile Tradition, Historical Archives

Except for pp. 25, 140, 143, 145, 146, 148, 149: Kevin Ash.

Every effort has been made to acknowledge correctly and contact the source and/or copyright holder of each picture, and Carlton Books Limited apologises for any unintentional errors or omissions which will be corrected in future editions of this book.